SHABBY CHIC®

SUMPTUOUS SETTINGS AND
OTHER LOVELY THINGS

ALSO BY
RACHEL ASHWELL

Shabby Chic

Rachel Ashwell's Shabby Chic
Treasure Hunting & Decorating Guide

The Shabby Chic Home

Shabby Chic: The Gift of Giving

RACHEL ASHWELL

SHABBY CHIC®

SUMPTUOUS SETTINGS AND OTHER LOVELY THINGS

PHOTOGRAPHS BY AMY NEUNSINGER

HARPER DESIGN
An Imprint of HarperCollinsPublishers

SHABBY CHIC: SUMPTUOUS SETTINGS
AND OTHER LOVELY THINGS.
Copyright © 2004 by Rachel Ashwell.
All rights reserved. Manufactured in China.
No part of this book may be used or reproduced in
any manner whatsoever without written permission except in
the case of brief quotations embodied in critical articles and
reviews. For information address Harper Design,
195 Broadway, New York, NY 10007.

HarperCollins books may be purchased for educational,
business, or sales promotional use.
For information please e-mail the Special Markets
Department at SPsales@harpercollins.com.

Published in 2014 by: Harper Design, *An Imprint of*
HarperCollins *Publishers*, 195 Broadway, New York, NY 10007
Tel: (212) 207-7000
Fax: (212) 207-7654
harperdesign@harpercollins.com

Distributed throughout the world by: HarperCollins
Publishers, 195 Broadway, New York, NY 10007

FIRST PAPERBACK EDITION published 2015.

Text by Claudia Vagt
Designed by Joel Avirom and Jason Snyder
Design assistant: Meghan Day Healey
Photograph on page 49 by Michael Caulfield WireImage

Library of Congress Cataloging-in-Publication Data

Ashwell, Rachel.
  Shabby chic : sumptous settings and other lovely
  things / Rachel Ashwell ; photographs by Amy
  Neunsinger.—1st ed.
    p. cm.
  ISBN 0-06-052393-X
    1. Dining rooms. 2. Interior decoration. 3. Entertaining.
  4. Table setting and decoration. 5. Party decorations.
  I. Title.
TX859.A83 2004
793.2—dc22

                                    2003058794

        ISBN 978-0-06-052394-7 (pbk.)

    15 16 17 18 19 SCP 10 9 8 7 6 5 4 3 2 1

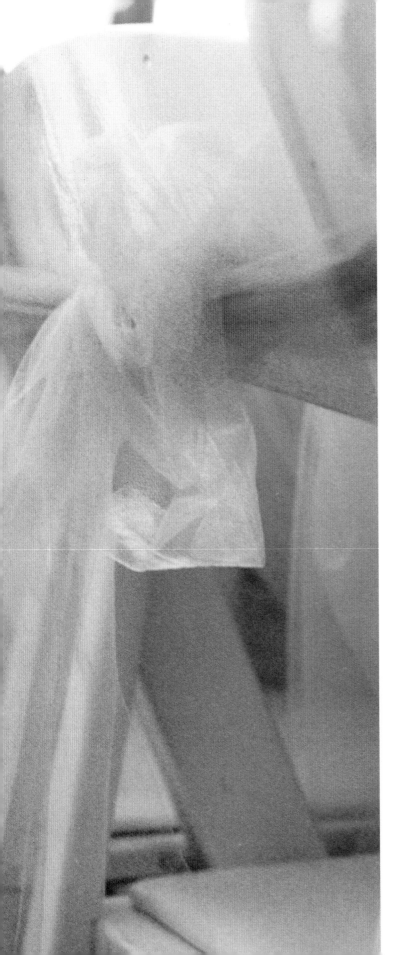

To Jake and Lily . . .
my other lovely things . . .

CONTENTS

ACKNOWLEDGMENTS

I would like to thank Judith Regan for her continued love of Shabby Chic. Thanks to Theresa Murphy for saying anything is possible. To Claudia Vagt for her patience with my words. To Amy Neunsinger for more glorious photography. To my sister, Deborah Greenfield, for her lovely, charming illustrations. For all my friends and associates—Pamela Anderson, Jennifer Lopez, Jenni and Sara, Jenni Jermyn, and Laurie Lynn Stark—for letting me be involved in such wonderful events in their lives. And finally, for my dear friend, Chelsy Reynolds, who inspired spontaneous beauty as only she could.

SHABBY CHIC®

SUMPTUOUS SETTINGS AND
OTHER LOVELY THINGS

INTRODUCTION

Creating a beautiful celebration is something that I really love to do, whether it's a child's birthday party or a charity gala. Whether the event is casual or formal, my goal is to treat my guests to a fabulous time in a sumptuous setting—a lovely environment that sets them at ease and brings out the joy in the occasion.

A sumptuous setting can be as simple as a tie-dyed sheet on the grass with a beach ball and a cupcake, or as elaborate as a sophisticated restaurant where every feature has been selected as if for a gracious private home.

Part of the enjoyment of entertaining family and friends is introducing them to new experiences. I look for interesting shops where I can discover new elements and new ideas. In Los Angeles, I avail myself of the wonderful collection of ethnic stores in the international downtown shopping area. There, treasures abound from all over the world—some to take home and some to just appreciate and be inspired by. The results are magical and surprisingly affordable. Few of the sumptuous settings in this book require a lot of money, just a lot of ingenuity.

This centerpiece was put together using a velvet-and-pearl pincushion, a small bunch of forget-me-nots, and a toy ballerina, complete with tutu.

OPPOSITE
I love the subtle colors of the flowers on the hat. They work nicely with the palette of the linens and bottles.

It's important for me, when I'm planning a celebration, to allow myself to use some fantasy elements as well as items with a sense of whimsy. Tinfoil stars, pastel feathers, and rhinestone tiaras all have a place in my world. I find that people of all ages love to indulge in flights of imagination—as at a baby shower where stylish young Californians can, for a moment, savor the delights of make-believe and play at being proper ladies, complete with vintage hats and parasols, at a tea in the English countryside.

To me, a sumptuous setting is a space that evokes abundance and generosity, the necessary backdrop for any party. This is easy to accomplish when you allow a love of beauty to be the foundation of your daily life.

Surrounding yourself with things you care about and find appealing means that you will be able to spontaneously pull together a celebration at any time from the stuff of your day-to-day existence.

A festive occasion in a sumptuous setting is a celebration of the spirit and the heart—a chance to show how much we care for the special people in our lives by pampering them a little, inspiring them a little, and allowing them to feel cherished—as they realize that every detail has been carefully thought through and arranged for their enjoyment. I find it enormously fulfilling to create these sumptuous settings full of lovely things.

1

NEW BEGINNINGS

BOUNTIFUL BABY SHOWERS

I didn't want to clutter my backyard with big umbrellas over the tables. I have a nice big tree, so I knew there would be some shaded areas and I didn't want to spoil the view. Instead, I hung some pretty parasols on the backs of the chairs. Along with the hats, the parasols' frilly, fluttery style made everyone feel very ladylike—as though we'd all just attended the races at Ascot. In addition to making a lovely picture, the parasols were very useful for those with delicate skin.

These diminutive eggs and feathers on the table are a special accent in any context, but at a baby shower, their symbolism of birth and new life makes them a natural decoration that is both subtle and casual.

As I walked around an arts-and-crafts supply store, I saw several Styrofoam signs with letters spelling out BABY SHOWER. I would never have thought of this myself, but something about it appealed to me. When I did my own version with pale blue paint, lavender glitter, and silver trim, it worked out beautifully. Moreover, it was very reasonable—under ten dollars.

As any mother knows, one reason it's enjoyable to give a baby shower is that you get to reconnect with all those baby things again. Seeing the little booties and blankets brings back so many memories. The other reason, of course, is that, for anyone, it's a lovely opportunity to honor the mother-to-be.

LAURIE'S
BABY SHOWER

BELOW AND OPPOSITE

A few traditional touches made it feel like a baby shower. The door banner was a whimsical introduction to the party. The vintage baby cup is a cherished piece I found long ago. So simple and so beautiful.

Laurie Lynn Stark is a dear friend of mine. She has fantastic style. She and her husband, Richard, have a company called Chrome Hearts that features amazing leather clothing and fabulous jewelry. Interestingly, many of the people who love Chrome Hearts also love Shabby Chic. Must be something intriguing about the combination of black leather and floral fabrics . . . I understand it, though. After all, my favorite outfit is a pair of jeans and cowboy boots!

Already a mom, Laurie was delighted when she discovered she was pregnant again. It was a bit of a surprise, however, when she found she was expecting not one baby but two. I think it's exciting any time a woman gets the news she's having a child. Nevertheless, there are probably some mixed emotions at the idea of twins. There is double the excitement, perhaps, but certainly also a sense of being a little overwhelmed— because two is a lot more than one.

Laurie and I have always shared an appreciation of all things English. I knew that if I were to create a traditional garden party for her, filled with all of my cherished vintage details, it would not be wasted upon her discriminating eye.

Therefore, I seized the chance to host a celebration and offered to make it a pretty day for her. I especially liked the idea of having a garden party. However, when you plan such a party you are at the mercy of nature, and I realized that I would have to design it with that in mind. My first concern was making sure my pastel palette wasn't washed out in the bright outdoor sunshine. I didn't want to go too pale with my greens, pinks, and blues. I augmented my usual color scheme with turquoise, fuchsia, and a strong blue. Even outside, these tones will hold their color.

I had recently received two rather large boxes of table linens with a lovely note saying the pieces were family heirlooms that the owner didn't quite know what to do with. She sent the linens to me, trusting me to come up with some purpose for them. I knew that the perfect opportunity to use them would arise eventually, so I was glad to have them.

As I wanted a strong palette for Laurie's party, I decided to dye some of the linens pink, some blue, and some green. Dyeing fabric is always a great adventure because there is no guarantee

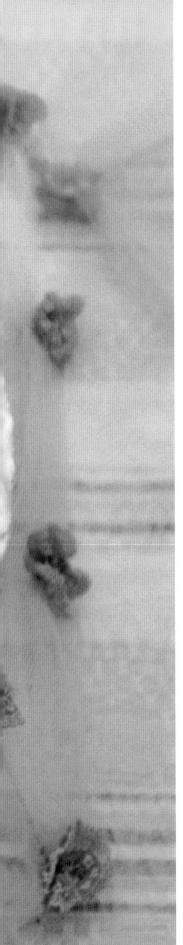

Delicate cake covers topped with vintage porcelain figurines give the delightful impression of elegant debutantes dressed in fanciful ball gowns.

A DECORATIVE CAKE COVER

 GET A PLAIN WIRE & NET CAKE COVER & DIP IN BASIN OF PINK, BLUE OR GREEN DYE TO LEND A PALE COLOR HUE TO THE NETTING.

 TAKE APPROXIMATELY 25 SHORT PIECES OF LACE TRIM & GATHER WITH A FEW STITCHES TO FORM LITTLE ROSETTES.

 DYE THESE DEEP HUES OF PINK, BLUE OR GREEN AND, WHEN DRY, GLUE ONTO THE CAKE COVER.

GLUE SEQUINS RANDOMLY TO EACH ROSETTE.

 GLUE A CERAMIC FIGURINE, SUCH AS THE PERFUME BOTTLE LADY HERE, ON TOP OF THE CAKE COVER.

13

When I happened upon these exquisite cameos in a flea market in Atlanta, the vendor claimed that they were made out of marble dust. It's a lovely thought. They make a wonderful finishing touch for the table.

A hodgepodge of napkins that had been sent to me as a gift were dyed pink, green, and a strong blue. Because I was dealing with all different types of lace, linens, and cottons, the result was not only a huge variety of color but also an incredible gradation of strong to light hues. The brightly colored napkins turned out so well that I decided to dye the lace the same way. Even though the lace came in all different sizes, it seemed like a great idea to treat all the pieces as doilies. So I put a little dyed lace doily at most of the thirty-five place settings.

how things will turn out, yet it is a fabulous process. Dyeing can cover a multitude of sins, from stains to mismatched fabrics to the everyday wear-and-tear of life. It can bring a fresh look to old worn linens and clothing with a minimum of effort. In addition, conventional items such as white sheets or plain mosquito netting can be transformed when dyed gorgeous, vivid colors. Commercial household dyes are conveniently found in grocery stores and drugstores and are fairly easy to use—just follow the directions on the packets and bottles. If you're not pleased with the results, you can in some cases undo the process with dye remover, but it's best to be open and adaptable to how the fabrics might turn out. In the case of my dyed napkins, I found the color variations caused by the different fabrics and laces to add to, rather than detract from, their charm.

THIS PAGE

For some young guests, seeing themselves in alluring little hats made the experience of "dress-up" a tantalizing glimpse into a future of grown-up glamour.

OPPOSITE

Guests took the hats found on their chairs and swapped until each had found a hat that felt right and went with her outfit. It was definitely something to talk about and, most important, really pretty and a lot of fun.

A turquoise headband adorned with silvery vintage flowers.

Overlapping pieces of light pink fabric give the illusion of layers of petals in this appealing hat.

Barely there, this delicate spray of tiny white flowers brushed with pink is exquisite.

Powder-blue flowers cover this cheerful hat like a flurry of pom-poms. A velvet bow and tulle band add spice.

The intense violet-blue color of these flowers ensures that only a few are needed to make a statement. The attached veil is the same vivid color.

One yellow bloom and a small white veil stand out beautifully on a subtle hat of overlapping petals in the most delicate hues of blue and white.

Fit for a ballerina, tiny cascades of white roses and daisies are attached to a leafy green circlet and interspersed with royal-blue ribbons.

Purple and lilac blooms grow in lush profusion on this headband.

A hat for a flirt. Bright lilac flowers clamber around a deep moss-green hat with a dark velvet crown. It's insouciance personified.

Ruffles and flourishes!
This engaging pink and white hat
does not take itself too seriously.

These dainty white flowers
seemed to have just blossomed
on their sage-green velvet
headband accented with a fawn-
colored bow.

Wispy feathers in a deep, vibrant
fuchsia gracefully set off the rosy
cloth petals of this elegant hat.

To me, this feminine hat has
distilled the essence of my favorite
pink roses. I love how the frothy
tulle crown emphasizes the lush
floppy roses.

A sheer veil of palest celadon
green drifts gently across a sprig
of muted flowers. Tiny pearl
edging lends a touch of luxury.

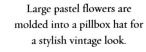

This hat, fashioned to resemble
one oversize white rose, radiates
a certain lavish simplicity.
It's gorgeous.

A pretty pillbox hat covered
in twisted lengths of spring
green tulle. The texture
is delicious.

Large pastel flowers are
molded into a pillbox hat for
a stylish vintage look.

This crushed tulle hat in deep rose
is enchanting with its pale gold
leaves, cherry-colored flowers, and
light pink veil.

TOP

An open raffia crown is embellished
with floppy white flowers for casual
perfection.

CENTER

Intricately woven ribbons in pink
and cream give the illusion of a flower
basket in this unusual hat.

BOTTOM

The warmth of a summer day is
captured in the golden blossoms
on this luscious hat.

OPPOSITE

A pearl-studded veil provides the
perfect contrast to this feathery blue hat.
The light, airy feel of the hat is delightful.

Baby showers are a nice excuse for women to get together. Not that a baby shower must be all-female, but many of them are. It's just a good opportunity to be a bit girlish, to say "ooh" and "ahh," to sit around laughing and chatting. I decided to take thorough advantage of this aspect at Laurie's party. I gathered some of my favorite props together, such as vintage hats and frilly parasols—the more feminine and dainty the better. I made them available to the guests so that we could all enjoy a bit of "dress-up" and play at being "ladies."

"Ladies," of course, have tea parties, and here are a few hints to make your tea party look authentic. The best china for this purpose tends to be English or French. Floral and traditional patterns work best. Use similar colors if possible, and feel free to mix colored china with white. A vintage cup on a white china saucer is lovely. If you've inherited china, now's the time to bring it out. Don't worry if some of the pieces aren't perfect.

RIGHT, OPPOSITE, AND FOLLOWING PAGE
I was delighted when the people who helped with the food arrived with china in various patterns. Some of the china wasn't necessarily what I'd choose, with its ivy and pansy patterns, and other patterns were a little bolder than I would have liked. However, it didn't really matter because the colorful overall look of this event made everything work together. It's gratifying to see that people are thinking outside of the box and realizing that not everything has to match.

At the last minute, Laurie decided we should have champagne. She had a beautiful hotel-style champagne bucket, and we put it out next to the flowers and the glassware. Though it happened that not even one bottle was ever uncorked, it didn't matter. The look of it alone was enough to justify its presence.

At the entrance to the party, I put out an old vintage baby book I'd had for a long time and inscribed it, "Words for the Stark family to welcome the new arrivals." Some of the guests wrote good wishes for Laurie while others penned words directly for the new babies. In either case, these words will be cherished keepsakes, a legacy for the twins.

To complete my theme of a traditional English garden party, I was determined to have a maypole. Laurie and I both relate to whimsical, feminine things, and I knew she would love it. Although I spent a lot of time visualizing the maypole, I have to admit that I had no idea at first how to go about creating one, so I promptly enlisted Theresa Murphy's help. I feel fortunate to work with Theresa because she is a wonderful craftsperson. There are no boundaries. I tell her what my dreams are, and not only does she creatively support my wishes, she does it very economically without sacrificing quality. When designing a party, feel free to imagine your most cherished scenario, whether you immediately know how to bring it about or not. If you need to, find an expert to help make your dream come true, and don't

just limit yourself to professional party planners—
consider asking art students, set designers,
carpenters, or people at the local crafts store.
Most people understand that the budget for a
private party has to be reasonable and are often
delighted to work on an original project that can
showcase their creativity.

In the end, it was a wonderful party with an
almost dreamlike quality to it. The vibrant colors
on the table glowed softly in the sunshine. The
"ladies" laughed and chatted in their pretty feminine
hats while twirling the lacy parasols. Many really
enjoyed the opportunity to be something of a little
girl again and play dress-up. Others, conversely,
were able to fantasize and catch a glimpse of another
more elegant self, in another time. A gentle wind
kept the maypole constantly in motion, so that
now and again guests would catch a glimpse of the
party through a ripple of pastel ribbons. It felt
enchanted, as unreal as if they were in a movie . . .
an English movie.

TOP AND CENTER
Beautiful leather handbags by Chrome Hearts.

BOTTOM
As a party favor, everyone received a Shabby Chic tote bag, which is
basically a small floral cotton bag. To give it some dimension, I
attached a vintage flower on top of the printed fabric flower with a
safety pin. In addition to being a very nice gift, the totes functioned
as yet more party trimming, adding another layer of flowers and
color to the decor.

I always take a final look at every table to make sure every detail is in place. I like to take a moment before a party to savor the setting, the flower arrangements, the colors, the carefully laid tables—the beauty of that moment of expectancy just before the guests arrive and everything is perfect, lovely, and waiting to be enjoyed.

Maypoles are part of an ancient European custom to celebrate the coming of spring. Some say the Romans brought the custom to England in celebration of the goddess Flora and, even today, many English villages put up maypoles at the beginning of May. I wanted this maypole to feel very springlike, with a slightly theatrical appearance. Since we didn't know yet whether Laurie's babies were going to be boys or girls, I decided that turquoise with pink accents would be a good color choice. My main requirements were a pole with ribbons coming from it and that turquoise crushed velvet be used.

MAYPOLE MATERIALS:

✦ ONE 8 FOOT 4×4 ✦ 16 2" L-BRACKETS & SCREWS ✦ 8 PIECES OF 2"×½" WOOD
✦ ONE SMALL LAZY SUSAN MECHANISM WITH HARDWARE ✦ THREE 3" WOOD SCREWS
✦ ONE 2' DIAMETER & ONE 1' DIAMETER 3/4" PLYWOOD CIRCLE
✦ ONE 24" POST SPIKE ✦ 15 YARDS OF VELVET ✦ PACKAGE OF QUILT BATTING
✦ STRAIGHT PINS ✦ SEQUINS SEED BEADS ✦ ABOUT 5 DOZEN MILLINER 3"
   FLOWERS, EITHER VINTAGE OR VINTAGE-LOOKING ✦ 6 YARDS OF SILVER
   BEADED GARLAND ✦ 8 SPOOLS OF 2" WIDE RIBBON-ASSORTED COLORS/TEXTURES
✦ TABLE SAW ✦ SCISSORS ✦ SEWING MACHINE ✦ SCREWDRIVER ✦ STAPLE GUN
✦ HOT GLUE GUN ✦ SLEDGE HAMMER ✦ WRENCH ✦ PLIERS

CONSTRUCTION:

✦ SET TABLE SAW BLADE AT 45° ANGLE. MARK 4×4 FIVE INCHES FROM BOTTOM. CUT POLE ALONG LENGTH AT 45° ANGLE ON ALL 4 EDGES TO THE 5" MARK. (OR HAVE THIS DONE AT A LUMBER STORE.)
✦ WRAP POLE (EXCEPT END POINT) IN QUILT BATTING & TACK IN PLACE WITH STAPLE GUN.
✦ CUT LENGTH OF VELVET 8'4" LONG BY 20" WIDE & SEW AN 8'4" TUBE.
✦ SLIP TUBE OVER POLE, SECURING AT THE TOP WITH STAPLES.
✦ CUT FOUR 2" WIDE × 9' LONG STRIPS OF VELVET & SET ASIDE.
✦ PUT A SEQUIN & SEED BEAD ON ABOUT 100 PINS ⟶
✦ USING THESE ATTACH THE 4 VELVET STRIPS TO THE TOP OF POLE, THEN WRAPPING & SECURING IT IN A BRAID PATTERN DOWN ITS LENGTH.
✦ COVER ONE SIDE PLUS THE EDGE OF BOTH THE 1' & 2' PLYWOOD CIRCLES WITH VELVET & TACK IN PLACE WITH STAPLE GUN.
✦ SCREW THE 1' CIRCLE TO POLE TOP WITH 3" WOOD SCREWS.
✦ BEND ALL 16 L-BRACKETS VELVET SIDE TO 120° ANGLE & SCREW 8 OF THESE EVENLY AROUND BACK SIDE OF 2' CIRCLE.
✦ SCREW THE 2' LENGTHS OF 2"×½" WOOD TO EACH BRACKET, REINFORCING WITH AN L-BRACKET ON THE BACK OF EACH PIECE.
✦ ALIGN LAZY SUSAN TO THE CENTER (THIS IS THE MAYPOLE CROWN.) OF THE CROWN, THEN MARKING & DRILLING THE HOLES.
✦ USING REMAINING VELVET, COVER THE OUTSIDE OF THE CROWN WITH STAPLE GUN, & STAPLE VELVET TO THE TOP OF ALL 8 PIECES OF WOOD.
✦ HOT GLUE FLOWERS AROUND BASE OF MAYPOLE CROWN. & IN CLUSTERS TO EACH OF THE CROWN POINTS.
✦ CUT 8 LENGTHS OF BEADED GARLAND, APPROX. 20" EACH. DRAPE & HOT GLUE TO BOTTOM EDGE OF FLORAL CLUSTERS.
✦ CUT 16 PIECES OF RIBBON TO DESIRED LENGTH & ATTACH 2 AT EACH OF THE CROWN POINT BASES.
✦ ATTACH LAZY SUSAN MECHANISM TO TOP OF POLE ON THE 1' CIRCLE.
✦ DRIVE POST SPIKE INTO DESIRED LOCATION & SECURE POST IN HOLDER
✦ WRAP POST HOLDER IN QUILT BATTING & PULL VELVET TUBE DOWN.
✦ CONTINUE POLES VELVET BRAIDING TO BASE.
✦ PLACE CROWN ON POLE & SECURE TO LAZY SUSAN.

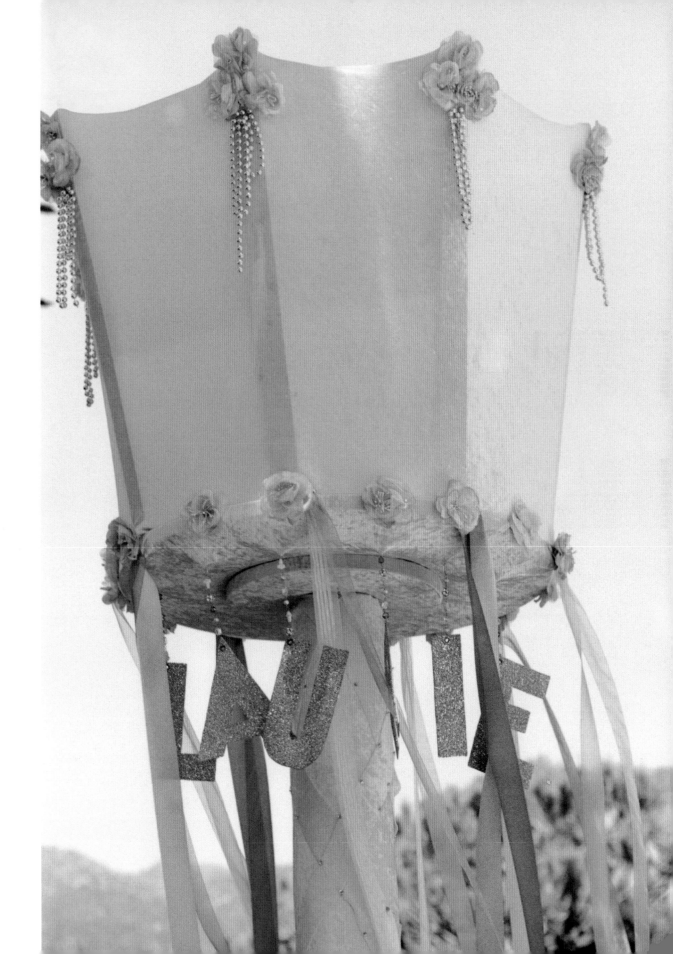

ABOVE

I particularly wanted garden roses for the flower
arrangements. Even though they don't last as long,
and you sometimes inherit spiders and other "guests,"
I wanted the flowers to look as if I'd just picked them
from the rosebushes.

OPPOSITE

I had a lovely old fan that had quite a few bits missing
from it, but there were about forty little spokes left and
they were all hand-painted with squiggles and flowers.
Inspired, I finally pulled the whole thing apart. I took all
these extra sticks, stuck them in a bowl with the flowers,
and popped a few shells in. The arrangements were rather
low but they had an eclectic feel to them, with a very
vintage, but nevertheless fresh, quality.

JENNI'S BABY SHOWER

Perhaps the nicest things about a mother's first baby shower, even though she doesn't realize it at the time, is that it's one of the last celebrations that's all about her—before she becomes, for the rest of her life, a mother. From then on, it's all about her child. It really is the end of one era and the beginning of another. Thus a baby shower is not just a celebration, it's a rite of passage. With that in mind, when I decided to give a baby shower for first-time mother-to-be Jenni Jermyn, I concentrated on making the celebration very personal, filled with sentimental gestures that honored this wonderful occasion—this new life that was about to commence for Jenni and her baby.

I wanted the party favor for the baby shower to be more than just a trifle for guests to take home—I hoped it would be a special memento for Jenni as well. I hand-made shadow boxes filled with traditional symbols of babies and new life. Personalized ribbons with Jenni's name and the date ensured that this keepsake was made especially for her. Many years from now, if she chooses, the little shadow box can be passed on to her child or grandchild and hold a real sense of meaning.

BELOW AND OPPOSITE
Don't overlook the tiniest possibility for decoration—such as these miniature bracelets and booties. The booties were slipped over the water bottles at the last minute but ended up being one of the most charming decorations.

I was inspired and rather touched by this small shadow box that I bought in an antiques mall. The little box was sitting on the shelf and evoked all these questions, such as Who made it, and why? I think it's delightful, even though it's a little cheesy. It's basically put together from a few odds and ends, including a bunch of flowers, a nylon butterfly with some sequins, and a box that's homemade-looking, with a cut-out doily. Still, there's something rather sweet about it, and it inspires lots of wonderful ideas.

It occurred to me that it would be enjoyable to create a picture frame with elements suitable for a baby shower. I found unfinished shadow boxes and painted them a creamy white. I made photocopies of a vintage baby print to use as the background.

Only a few pretty elements are needed to create
the baby shower picture frame. Silver lace was
glued around the edge of the print with a glue
gun. Then soft, powder-blue feathers, creamy
lace, and tiny papier-mâché eggs from a craft-
supply house were attached as well, along with
sparkling rhinestones and small baby buttons.
The last touches were little ribbons printed
with Jenni's name and the words "baby shower."
By personalizing it with that little bit of ribbon,
I made the box that much more meaningful for
Jenni and her family.

New moms need many practical things, but most of all they cherish items that honor and symbolize this special time in their lives. I deliberately chose gifts for Jenni that had a lasting quality—gifts whose beauty would deepen over time and that she could keep forever, treasuring them in years to come as "the first diaper bag," "the first baby bowl." Given my love for vintage, that seemed to be the perfect path to take. However, I was a little restricted, since I had to avoid anything that wasn't completely clean or that contained dangerous elements such as lead paint or sharp edges. Nevertheless, it was important to me, and I persevered until I found exactly what I wanted—items with an heirloom quality, not just utilitarian plastic things that would soon be outgrown or used up.

With her personalized shadow-box memento and vintage gifts to remind her, I hope Jenni will always fondly recall everyone gathering for this last celebration before her new life with her new baby began.

ABOVE

As a gift for the mom-to-be, I happened upon a lovely old sewing bag that will work perfectly well for diapers. Once you have a baby, you always need a bag to carry things around, whether toys, bottles, or clothes.

OPPOSITE

Before the guests left, they took the time to leave a message for Jenni in this vintage baby book. It's a final memento for Jenni of everyone's thoughts and good wishes for her, written down for her to keep. The feather pen was another tempting opportunity to use one of my favorite accents.

ABOVE

I found a lovely vintage bowl at an antiques shop that is the perfect baby gift. There are absolutely no chips or cracks, so I can be sure it's hygienic enough for a baby to use.

RIGHT TOP, BOTTOM, AND OPPOSITE

I am always on the lookout at flea markets and antiques malls for vintage prints with my themes. Sweet drawings of flowers, little birds, ribbons, and so forth are all collectibles for me. Many also contain sentimental sayings and quotes. A customer sent me these vintage baby prints from an old baby book she found. She wasn't sure what to do with them but thought I might enjoy them. So I popped them on the shelf and thought, *One day* . . . When I began planning Jenni's shower, it seemed the perfect time to pull them out. The miniature feel of the baby announcement card appealed to me, and I adapted the design for the party invitation.

2

HOME AWAY FROM HOME

MADRE'S:
JENNIFER LOPEZ'S
EXQUISITE
RESTAURANT

One day, I got a call from Jennifer Lopez's assistant saying that Jennifer was

thinking of opening a restaurant in Pasadena, California, and would like to meet with me.

She had been especially inspired by an episode of my television series, *Rachel Ashwell's Shabby Chic,*

in which I renovated a house in Santa Monica for my parents. It resonated with Jennifer

because she was planning to renovate an existing restaurant for members of her own family.

After watching the show, she decided that my style philosophy was the perfect way to approach

her restaurant.

I was intrigued by the prospect. Though I'd never designed a restaurant before, I certainly

could relate to the idea of creating a beautiful space in a way that was both effective and economical.

During our initial meeting in Los Angeles, Jennifer explained how she imagined her

restaurant might look. She envisioned the place as Cuban, sexy, and romantic. Listening, I

couldn't help thinking of lots of red, a very hot and vibrant atmosphere, with pillows on the

floor and a lively, salsa flavor. It would be a challenge to incorporate my favorite choices of pastel

colors and delicate roses into all of this.

The entrance to Madre's. I found an iron chandelier, painted it white, and had it wired for outdoor use. Simple and elegant, vintage garden urns are the only other ornaments needed.

Not only would the concept test my creativity, but so would the logistics. As with the Santa Monica house, I wouldn't have a lot of time or money to work with—just five weeks and a really tight budget.

I have to confess, actually, that that was fine with me. I work better with a few limitations. If I'd had a million dollars and six months to complete the job, I honestly would have found it more overwhelming. An unlimited amount of money gives you no boundaries. A few constraints make it easier to decide where to go and what to get. They make me focus, and I find that helpful.

It's a good approach when redoing a room on a budget, which almost all of us have to do at one point or another. Instead of seeing it as a limitation, use your budget as a way to concentrate your efforts. Don't waste time worrying about extravagances you can't afford; enjoy experimenting with all the possibilities that are available at any level with imagination. I find that a little creativity wins over throwing money at a project every time.

Everyone wants to know what Jennifer is like. She is, of course, as pretty and glamorous as you might imagine, but she's also very businesslike. She let me know from the outset that if I wanted to take on the project, my attention to detail would be greatly appreciated; it would not be wasted on her. I realized that one of the reasons she's had such a multifaceted career is that she really pays attention to the details of every single element she's involved in.

I liked her and knew I could work with her. It was important that we have a good rapport, especially under such a deadline and with a tight budget. However, before either of us committed to anything, we decided to look at the actual site together.

A few days later, I met Jennifer at the restaurant, which had originally been a very well known, very conservative and gentlemanly restaurant in Pasadena, which itself is a very traditional town. My first impression was of dark wood and drab paneling, with little light. All I could imagine, actually, were businessmen smoking cigars—very prim and proper, nothing sexy about the place at all.

The more Jennifer and I explored the restaurant, however, the more her vision became clear to me. The gloomy bar area had great bones and the right proportions to become a festive venue. And although the booths along the wall were tired and dilapidated, they nevertheless had the potential to become rich, intimate settings for romantic dinners. Bland and boring, the main dining room could be revitalized with some creative touches, and once the small private dining area was set off to its best advantage, it would be the perfect VIP retreat.

Now that I had some sense of the overall picture, it was time to go off, think about it for a few days, and come back with some ideas. Years of experience have taught me to allow all the images and first impressions of a room or any interior space to drift through my mind for a while. I let anything that catches my attention inspire me without editing myself at first. The color of a flower, a picture in a magazine, bright baubles at the flea market—anything can spark an idea. Books are always a great resource. I went to some bookstores, sat down, and looked at everything I could find—books on travel, architecture, and design—that might relate to the subject of Cuban style.

Jennifer Lopez on the opening night of Madre's.

COMIDA LATINA

MADRE'S

ESTABLISHED 2002

My research paid off. I was delighted to find a kind of Cuban decor that very much lends itself to my approach. Known as Old Havana style, it favors a classic, almost European elegance of cracked walls, with patinas of cream and hues of green. I was particularly inspired by historical photographs of Havana during the early part of the last century. Whether depicting a modest row of houses or the most opulent mansions, the pictures show gracious homes that combine the best of a sultry island sensibility with Old World charm. Some houses are simple, with the subdued colors of sun-washed rooms that hold a few chairs and a worn table. Other more elaborate interiors display crystal chandeliers gleaming off silver place settings on crisp white linens. The look was enchanting, and I began to envision an elegant atmosphere that was more about texture than color.

Equipped with all these fascinating photos, I went back to Jennifer and explained how they had inspired my vision for the restaurant as a lively yet gracious place to dine. She loved them. One of the things she had said repeatedly was that she wanted to feel as if she were going to her grandmother's house when entering the restaurant, and these photos captured the mood exactly. In fact, Jennifer planned to name the restaurant "Madre's" to reinforce that feeling of home.

Undertaking such a big job requires organization. To begin, I separated the project into roughly five different areas: Seating, Lighting and Mirrors, Fabric and Lace, Place Settings, and Flowers and Final Touches. Each category had its special challenges and rewards. This is the way I suggest approaching a home renovation as well. Divide the work into different categories and make a plan for each so that you don't get overwhelmed.

OPPOSITE
The rich look of a Cuban cigar box inspired the design of the menu. A vintage print of a senorita and her suitor in the 1930s adds a festive and fun touch. These menus set the standard for the extraordinary attention to detail and authenticity that is found throughout the restaurant.

ABOVE
Every night, the staff replenishes these simple votives on a clear glass shelf. I wanted them to go almost unnoticed— just a subtle effect of shimmering flames that was more a feeling than anything else. I found it so beautiful that now I do this in my own home as well.

SEATING

BELOW

Soft beige velvet on an off-white reproduction Louis XVI chair was the perfect combination for the VIP room. The plush button back exudes luxury. The chair is fitted with a ruffled Shabby Chic slipcover in linen, which was placed on all the chairs in the restaurant for practicality. The slipcovers also tie together the differing versions of the chairs used throughout the restaurant.

RIGHT

The main dining room at Madre's is designed to allow gracious dining in lovely surroundings. Formal without being stuffy, it is quietly beautiful with a classical aura of tradition and timeworn elegance. A gleaming gold-framed mirror indicates the elegant VIP room just beyond.

The single most challenging element of the job was seating. I knew that I needed close to two hundred restaurant-quality chairs. They had to be sturdy but comfortable, utilitarian yet graceful. This challenge put my personal philosophy of beauty, comfort, and function to the ultimate test, because I was determined not to compromise.

It was also important that I find them as soon as possible, because these chairs were going to be critical in establishing a sense of flow in the restaurant. Each area—the bar, the main dining room, and the VIP room— had to function in concert with the others. I needed to tie them together, but in a way that maintained their individuality. At Madre's, the chairs were an important way to achieve this sense of unity. My first choice was a beautiful Louis XVI reproduction. It came in several similar variations that were different enough to give each one character. Unfortunately, there was a six-month lead time involved in ordering these chairs from France. A frantic search ensued until I discovered an Italian version that was a more than acceptable substitute. Moreover, the chairs were immediately available.

Another lovely cane-backed settee that helps make Madre's feel more like a beautiful home than a restaurant. One of my favorite design accessories is the throw pillow. These are splendid examples. Made of taffeta, brocade, linen, and needlepoint, each pillow is finished with a tasseled trim. The fresh oyster linen used on the seat cushion is a serene contrast to their ornate look.

OPPOSITE

A luxurious booth in the bar. Rich chenille curtains can be drawn for an intimate meal beneath a vintage chandelier. The smocking detail at the top of the curtains is expensive but worth it. Details are important, and I like to add domestic touches whenever possible in a public or corporate environment. These make the restaurant feel like a beautiful home. The curtain rings, tiebacks, and poles are all made of aged brass. Cream-colored booths may not be the most practical choice, yet I felt a feminine touch was needed to balance the mood of the dark wooden bar.

I chose to scatter several sofas and settees throughout the restaurant. I love this look, and this type of seating arrangement is great for the home as well. It's more interesting and functional. Unconventional combinations of seating help to break up the space in a fresh way and offer friends and family a different way to interact with each other. There is nothing more romantic than sitting down to dinner with your spouse at a table with a French settee. Benches can be a lot of fun for children, and practical for squirmy little ones who are constantly getting up and down. The way you group your chairs, tables, and sofas has a great influence in setting a mood that fosters warmth and easy conversation. In addition, these variations are what give a home's decor its individuality.

LIGHTING AND MIRRORS

I was told that one of the reasons the last restaurant on this site did not do well was because the unattractive lighting made everybody look ugly, and no one wanted to come back. The issue of how to help everyone in the restaurant look fabulous became an important one.

Lighting is an extremely important element in determining the ambience of a room. Beautiful furniture and accessories wither under harsh white or fluorescent light, while lighting that is too dim creates a murky, unpleasant atmosphere. When the right balance is achieved, the lighting will radiate a flattering aura that brings out the beauty in any room and in any person.

LEFT

A French candelabra is filled with plain white candles in small clear glass votives. The look is striking and complements the large mirror that in turn reflects the amber drops of the chandelier. I love the visual layering of texture, detail, and richness—to me that exemplifies elegance.

OPPOSITE

Damask sofas in a soft taupe-brown help create a look of home in this cozy seating area near the bar at Madre's. I added matching arm sleeves for protection and plopped down a few antique embroidered pillows for an extra personal touch. The pale, carved mantel was a flea market treasure and a huge improvement over the severe unadorned fireplace that had been there before. I was lucky that the measurements of the mantel and the fireplace matched perfectly and required no alterations. Mantels are a lovely fixture to buy at flea markets and transform, but they do have the drawback of having already been sized. In some instances, you can cut down a mantel that is too big. Alternatively, you can fill the gap with a marble or tile surround in the fireplace. Although, if the dimensions of the mantel are too small, don't bother buying the piece, however lovely. It won't work, as the parts of the mantel exposed to the fireplace opening will always be a fire hazard. The coffee table is actually a beautifully carved and heavily painted door. I transformed it into a table by placing it on ready-made turned wooden legs and finishing it off with a glass top.

The chandeliers were specially designed to be no longer than twenty-four inches because of the low ceiling. This ensured enough headroom for all the guests—even very tall ones like Shaquille O'Neal. As lovely as chandeliers are, they provide only so much light. Therefore, for practical purposes I used the existing pin lights to enhance the chandelier lighting and provide more illumination in a subtle way. It worked so well that I reproduced the exact arrangement in my own home.

BOTTOM

One of the three vintage chandeliers used over the booths in the bar. Amber drops give a warm, flattering glow to the light emanating from the chandelier. Typically, I prefer crystal drops that are pale pink or turquoise. However, Jennifer had mentioned to me that when she is lit for the stage or movies she finds an amber hue flattering to her skin. I was in favor of anything that might improve the lighting, especially in a restaurant where people go to have a good time and want to look nice. I had a few chandeliers made with amber drops for the dining room as well—again, just to help tie these rooms together.

OPPOSITE TOP AND CENTER

I love the combination of crystal globe fixtures with traditional hanging chandeliers. The light fixture in the bar is a focal point, so I found a vintage one whose beads, with their aged finish, gave the lighting a timeworn elegance worth gazing at. Pin lights set off its magnificence and help illuminate the beautiful tin ceiling as well.

OPPOSITE BOTTOM

To give some dull sconces that came with the restaurant a second chance, I designed new shades in a silvery silk that gave a completely fresh look, and the sconces became a graceful addition to the lighting. In this case, the subtle interplay of color and texture among the pewter-green Venetian plaster walls, the muted silver sconces, and the silky tasseled shades gives the rooms character.

Lighting fixtures should be as pleasing to the eye as the light shining from them. In my opinion, the most beautiful of all lighting fixtures is the chandelier—a necessity in my world. Sparkling light is what makes a chandelier special. There is nothing worse than a dirty, dull chandelier! A chandelier cleaner, found at lighting stores, makes it easy. Just spray it on, lay a cloth on the floor underneath to catch the drips, and that's it. Not only does a spotlessly clean chandelier create a wonderful aura, but it also inspires romance by making everyone look good.

I worked out that I needed about thirty chandeliers for Madre's. Not only were they suitably glamorous, but the existing tin ceiling would provide a magnificent backdrop. Although I planned to hang only a few strategically placed vintage chandeliers and use reproductions for the rest, this definitely affected the budget. However, I strongly felt that the drama and practicality of these lights made them indispensable.

It was important to use as much of the existing electrical wiring and fixtures as possible. I knew that if I started changing electrical outlets things could become very expensive very quickly. As sometimes happens, however, necessity proved to be unexpectedly rewarding. The existing fixtures in Madre's that initially seemed dull or even ugly were transformed, with a little imagination. Pin lights in the ceiling were, to my mind, unattractively modern, almost corporate-looking, although it would cost a fortune to remove them. When I looked at them in a different way, however, as a means to augment the softer light of the chandeliers, the pin lights suddenly acquired a real practicality, and I happily kept them in place. Apply some imagination to any inherited fixtures before tossing them out. Put glaring track lighting or recessed lighting on a dimmer switch. Try painting the fixtures a different color. New shades

can dramatically change the appearance as well. Look in the Yellow Pages to find lamp shade makers who will do custom work. They're not hard to find and the rewards are gratifying.

Know when and where to spend your money to greatest effect. In my home, I put the money for lighting fixtures in areas that I sit in, that I ponder in. I use more affordable lighting in the transitional areas. That doesn't mean there should be something ugly in the foyer, but the chandelier that you look at from the table *has* to be beautiful.

To help the lighting, I changed the dark walls at Madre's into a lovely pale shade of silvery green using a Venetian plaster process. Color is mixed into the plaster before it is applied to the walls to give an authentic feel and texture, unlike the more common rag-faux painting method. The ceilings were painted with a shiny gloss to reflect the chandeliers I planned to install. It's a great solution for any drab drywall ceiling, as it gives the illusion of authentic plaster.

Mirrors are obviously important when you're trying to reflect light in a space. Yet I don't like mirror tiles or large floor-to-ceiling sheets of mirrored glass. I find the effect overwhelming and cold. I want an intimate, romantic look, and that, to me, is only achieved with individual mirrors. There are so many beautiful options. Some ornate mirrors encased in gold-leaf frames adorned with carved flowers and ribbons are virtual masterpieces. I often like to hang several mirrors in one area for a subtle sense of depth, because the reflections are broken up a bit and you catch just a glimpse of an image here and there. I also make sure to place mirrors where they will reflect the things I love. Vibrant flowers, glowing candles, and twinkling chandeliers can all be placed so that their likenesses are echoed in a lovely way by the mirror.

TOP

A vintage mirror with a deep beveled frame. I hung twenty-five individual mirrors throughout Madre's at the same height to add depth and light without the commercial wall-to-wall look common to many restaurants. They also reflect the glittering lights and crystals of the chandeliers to great advantage.

BOTTOM

A beveled mirror from the 1940s and simple sconces offset the striped wallpaper in the men's bathroom. The existing utilitarian soap pump was left in place, something I had to live with for practical reasons. However, that's part of life, and I prefer to embrace this piece as a considered imperfection. It's grounding and keeps the room from being too precious. Still, I couldn't resist leaving my own little design signature with this porcelain vase and flowers.

OPPOSITE

More than any other room, a bathroom gives you the excuse to go a little over the top when you decorate. After all, it's where you primp, preen, and make yourself beautiful. A bathroom invites extravagant appointments, such as this painting that I call *The Pretty Lady*. Of all the pictures I've purchased, it's one of my favorites. Here, she provides a touch of glamour in the ladies' bathroom at Madre's. Soft pink rose wallpaper and a delicate upholstered chair are other thoroughly feminine elements that make restaurant guests feel pampered.

62

For Madre's I chose a collection of vintage mirrors from the 1940s. Unframed, some of them were scalloped while others were rectangular or oval, but they all had a beveled edge. I hoped that because they all were of a similar size and theme, it would feel that there had been a rhyme and reason in placing them. I soon learned to love these mirrors and bought many more of them than I needed. Now we have those mirrors in the store and, among the staff, they're known as the "J.Lo" mirror.

FABRIC AND LACE

I'm not a big curtain person, but with the restaurant's five large exterior windows, countless interior windows, and several French doors, I ended up buying more than four hundred yards of fabric.

It's not a coincidence that I've made designing my own Shabby Chic fabrics a priority. Fabrics are one of the easiest ways to create a lovely look in any room, public or private.

The fabrics in Madre's had to serve several functions. They had to be beautiful and elegant, of course, but they also had to be sturdy. Linen and chenille were natural choices, yet I was determined to find a place for lace. Lace is a favorite of mine, but because it's expensive and delicate, there were only a few places in Madre's that I could actually find a home for it. I used it to great advantage in the VIP room as a kind of flirty, ruffled underskirt that peeked out beneath the linen tablecloths. Layering and unexpected touches of exquisite detail are a vital part of my style that I enjoy implementing because it evokes a pleasant sense of discovery. Surprisingly, another opportunity to use lace turned up in the bar, which, with its signature *Mojito* cocktails and salsa bands, is a sultry, enticing area. Putting a bit of lace in with a party crowd is a potential nightmare. However, I positioned lace runners on all of the tables and then put a piece of glass on top, so the lace was visible but protected.

ABOVE
Lace napkins ensured that even the breadbasket would have a personal touch. The china salt and pepper shakers are vintage. They're rarely seen these days, and I considered them a real find.

OPPOSITE
Unconventional seating like this French settee adds interest and breaks up the monotonous look of rows and rows of chairs. A sumptuous Aubusson pillow adds comfort. I had decided on straightforward white linen tablecloths and napkins, but for extra detail and special interest, I made what I call white petticoats that go underneath the linen just to give that little feminine fluff. Jennifer loved the eyelet lace ruffles on the tablecloths. They reminded her of one of her stage outfits. Both Jennifer and I believe attention to detail makes all the difference.

PLACE SETTINGS

As in your home, the basics are critical for a restaurant. Plates, china, glassware, and cutlery—all make an indelible first impression on your guests. For the restaurant, most of the place settings would have to be sturdy commercial ware for practical reasons. Still, I wanted Madre's to keep the feeling of home, with at least one decorative vintage plate at each setting. Even so, that relatively modest requirement meant that I had to find close to two hundred plates of various sizes.

I also wanted all sugars, creamers, teapots, and vases to be vintage. They make a dramatic statement and are used sparingly. Although I required only a few of these pieces for each table, they certainly added up quickly, both financially and in volume.

Finding hundreds of vintage china items within the budget and time frame I'd committed to was really a task. I went to every antiques mall and flea market possible during the next five weeks. I would pick up nearly every creamer or sugar bowl that had a pink flower on it. Nevertheless, if it didn't feel authentic, I left it behind. What were my criteria? Nothing past the 1930s for the most part, and I tended to stay with classic china made in France. Of course, I passed on any chipped or broken pieces. Normally I stay away from complete dinner sets. Mix-and-match is essential for my look. In this case, however, it was tempting to be able to pick up so many pieces at once. I just made sure that the restaurant staff combined them with other china patterns on the tables.

BELOW
Spicy Cuban favorites are a lively contrast to the vintage china.

OPPOSITE
A place setting at Madre's. No two are alike, thanks to my mix-and-match way of thinking. This one consists of a mercury vase, cut-glass goblets, and fine French china, guaranteed to make any meal a treat.

Of all the vintage elements that I purchased, Jennifer really appreciated these things the most. The night before we opened, we viewed every single piece of vintage china together. Jennifer played with them like a girl in a dollhouse all night long. She kept putting this plate with that saucer, this vase . . . I left her there at eleven o'clock at night, and she was still playing with the china.

Jennifer really has an eye for beauty, detail, and authenticity. Had I just gone to some china company and had them put a load of floral detail on some plates, she would have been disappointed. Instead, she treasures these pieces.

FLOWERS AND FINAL TOUCHES

Of course, any space I decorate must incorporate flowers. Too often restaurant flowers are either sad nylon daisies in a little vase or a huge bouquet that arrives once a week—some mixture of calla lilies and birds-of-paradise. Neither of those fit into my vision for Madre's. I wanted it to feel as if Jennifer's grandmother had gone into the backyard, picked a few little roses, and flung them in a vase. No more than two rosebuds per table—not a big deal. However, in the bar area, which had heavy chenille curtains and a smokier feeling, I put orangey, rust-colored roses, which are actually less expensive.

I bought only five oil paintings of muted pink roses set in old gold frames. Not valuable, they're still decorative. I feel they are definitely something Grandmother would have had on her walls, and so I found strategic places, for these paintings here

OPPOSITE
Small vintage elements such as this enamel box adorn every table.

TOP
One of my favorite color combinations— turquoise and silver—is reflected in this small glass vase set off to its best advantage on one of the white wicker tables in the patio. A pretty doily has been slipped between the glass top and the table for a delicate effect.

ABOVE
This birdbath was a flea-market find. I filled it with white sand to serve as an ashtray outside the entrance to the restaurant. Always be open to alternative uses for any treasure.

and there. Although rose paintings are a signature part of my design, I felt the environment at Madre's required more variety, and I enjoyed exploring other options. The experience gave me the opportunity to add other themes, such as portraits and Latin-inspired artwork, to my repertoire.

I do think this whole restaurant is glorious to look at. Eye candy is important. There's nothing in Madre's that wasn't thought about and carefully addressed. Looking at beautiful things makes me feel that my life has a thoughtful quality to it— that the things around me have been selected; that my world's not arbitrary.

I buy for my stores all the time. Although I've been doing it for twelve years, only rarely do I find something that I want to keep. However, I was so obsessed and impassioned by this particular project that I found quite a few items I truly adored. These pieces were very difficult for me to let go of, as they were very special and very beautiful. Nevertheless, I relinquished them with a certain professional satisfaction. After I finished my work, I walked away from Madre's thinking that, as far as my decorating talents go, this was just about as good as it gets.

A tiny arrangement of flowers
adds a grace note wherever it's put—
such as here on the hostess stand.

ne of the hundreds of vintage pieces
d to find within a few weeks in order
o make our opening-day deadline.

The delicate ornamentation of this
vase needs only a single flower
to complement it.

A creamer used as a sugar bowl has
great charm. Gold and other bright
colors lend a Spanish flair.

A vintage creamer's primitive
ountry rose design works just as well
as more delicate patterns.

I love china creamers. They speak to me of another
far more gracious era where every detail mattered.
Luckily for me, sugar substitutes are packaged in
pastel colors that fit right in with my palette!

This creamer has a small china lid that's
perfectly proportioned. That, plus the tiny
flower garlands, makes it feel like something
out of a dollhouse.

An eclectic collection of rose-filled vases
waiting to adorn the tables in the dining room.
They're all that's needed. Anything more
elaborate would be distracting and pretentious.

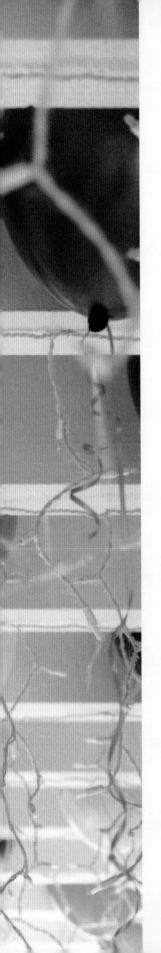

3

TURQUOISE PARTY TIME

HAPPY BIRTHDAY DELIGHTS

PREVIOUS SPREAD
Balloons were let loose to float up to the ceiling. Against the white beams, the colorful balloons and streamers created a cheery atmosphere.

OPPOSITE
As Pamela and I made our way outside, I started to feel my turquoise creation wobble and sway. . . . I couldn't quite believe it was happening, but before we reached the outside table, the plastic pillars supporting each tier holding the cupcakes systematically collapsed, one by one. . . . Oh well! We salvaged what cakes we could . . . and then had a laugh.

Pamela Anderson and I first met casually, as neighbors in Malibu. As I got to know her, I found that as different as we are in many ways, we share a surprising number of similarities. Pamela has a real affinity for style and detail. Our children are high priorities in our lives. She's a good mom and an involved one. She takes beautiful photographs of her two sons, Brandon and Dylan, that are displayed around her home. It was easy for me to relate to this. As single moms, Pamela and I make sure that our children and homes come first. We instinctively recognized this in each other and became friends.

I was not surprised, then, when she wanted to plan a party that was different and special for Brandon's sixth birthday. She didn't just want to get pizza and order a bunch of balloons. Nor did she want to spend a fortune.

Pamela asked me if I could help her decorate for the party. As we talked, I realized that, at the end of the day, it would cross over into a grown-up party as well. Pamela lives at the beach. When parents drop their young kids off for a party, it's easier for them to hang around, rather

than drive the long distance home and then come back to pick them up. Therefore, as we planned the party, I kept in mind that the setting, although for the kids, was also going to be used and appreciated by adults as well.

Pamela's house is very pretty, with white, airy rooms and pastel-colored vintage furniture in a casual setting. I didn't have to change a lot. The look of the house reflects how she lives. It's attractive, festive, and fun. All I had to do was embellish it. Everything in her house is lovely and functional and could easily be used to create a lively celebration.

As often happens, I started my preparations by establishing a color scheme. Pink wasn't going to work because the party was for boys, and besides, Pamela's very fond of blue and turquoise tones. I decided that, considering the beach environment, a range of turquoise and green shades would work well. That settled, I began to pull my elements together.

LEFT

If you are determined, you can make any color scheme work—no matter how improbable it might seem at first to be able to find turquoise candy.

RIGHT

Turquoise Jell-O, too . . . why not?

OPPOSITE

I wanted the presentation of the cupcakes to be a bit extravagant and ornate, almost a kid's version of a wedding cake. I'd found a formal, three-tiered cake plate and we painstakingly arranged the cupcakes together inside the house. I was proud of my fantastic turquoise construction.

Because Pamela has a tiny kitchen, everything revolves around her porch, which is used for entertaining and treated like a regular room. A chandelier has been hung for lighting and the chain covered with ruched fabric. Underneath is a lovely table surrounded by mismatched chairs. Antique harvest tables like this are rare now because appreciation of their beauty and utility has risen. They're favorites of mine because of the sense of history they convey. I like to think of all the meals that have been served and all the conversations that have taken place around tables like this one. Like the cabinet, it's a lovely vintage piece that nevertheless has enough wear and tear to work outside where any effects of the California weather will only add to the table's beauty. Pamela and I share the same palette. Her choices in decor naturally harmonize with mine, so it was easy for me to embellish her house for the party.

I also came up with the idea of using carnations rather than more traditional flowers like floppy pink roses or peonies. Carnations are a nice, youthful flower that are very affordable and can go a long way. They don't come in the turquoise shade I wanted for the color palette, so I dyed them.

These days, some children's parties are so overplanned that the kids really just end up being spectators. At Brandon's party, the kids were encouraged to play with each other. We kept a few incidental props within easy reach, such as some hats on a hook and some beach balls to toss around. Less really is more—it was an easygoing, fun party that I think the kids really enjoyed. The hats were a particular hit. As the children left for home, each child was given a box of modest gifts that were long on imagination and short on expense. I hope it will remind them of a lovely afternoon and a birthday party designed for children of all ages.

TOP

I collect small turquoise vases whenever I can find them. For the most part, they're a wonderful color for my palette of pale flowers. In this case, I used them for a touch of fantasy and whimsy. Gathered together in a group like this, they are exquisite.

BOTTOM AND OPPOSITE

I made this wreath from hand-dyed carnations. It's easy—just stick the carnations into a Styrofoam ring. These rings can be bought in various sizes at an arts-and-crafts store. The larger the ring and the more carnations, the better the effect—so feel free to be lavish. The variations of turquoise shades that the dyed flowers display give a lovely textured quality. The wreath has been propped up for an informal feel against a fabulous cabinet. Originally a built-in cupboard, the piece has been resurrected as a beautiful freestanding piece of furniture. While of good quality, the finish is distressed enough that the piece can be used outdoors without worry. To me, a perfect finish is one that shows the passage of time in peeling paint and worn surfaces but is not so damaged as to seem dilapidated or grubby.

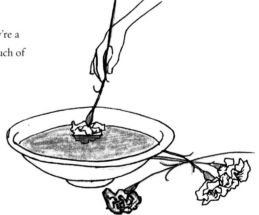

GENTLY DIP EACH FLOWER IN COLD DYE LIQUID.

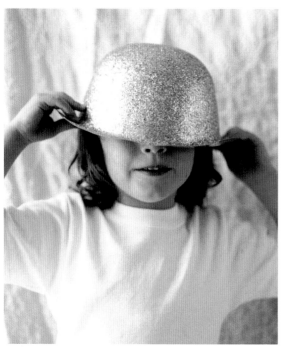

The simplest things give the greatest joy.

TOP

Sparkling plastic jewels make these glasses memorable.

BOTTOM

A rented table wrapped in aluminum foil is kid-friendly, affordable, and functional. The reflective surface of the table is the perfect backdrop for pale lemonade and dark blue water bottles. Plastic glasses sparkle with tiny glued-on jewels bought at an arts-and-crafts store and are complemented by the small foil stars scattered about the table. Hydrangeas, one of my favorite flowers, surround the table. Their deep blue and lilac hues complement my turquoise-and-silver color scheme. I love all the colors here; they are a bit on the intense side of my color palette, yet everything still looks fresh and luminous.

OPPOSITE

Balloons and streamers have to be one of the easiest and most efficient ways to decorate for a party. Have fun with the colors and you're halfway there.

TOP AND BOTTOM

Party favors. Aluminum takeout containers were tied up with plain string for the boys, while the girls' were wrapped with a pale blue ribbon. They were filled with little presents like silver space alien antenna headgear, fun pencils, and a bit of candy—all color-coordinated to go with our party theme. A Polaroid was taken of each child, and that was part of their gift to take home.

LEFT

Food cans from foreign countries are amusing containers for straws and other plastic cutlery. They're often found in specialty grocery stores. I loved the colorful graphics on these fruit cans in complementary tones of peach and yellow and found them to be the perfect contrast to set off our forks, spoons, and straws.

LEFT

A few simple elements can have a remarkably big effect. Consider this gathering of silvery almond candies, blue starfish, and frilly carnations in a turquoise glass vase—it's effortlessly lovely.

BELOW

I went to a restaurant supply company and got some aluminum takeout food containers, and mixed them with some regular plastic blue and turquoise paper plates. These kinds of containers are great for a party or picnic where kids are running around because they ensure that the sandwich, or whatever the children are eating, stays on the plate.

OPPOSITE

Starfish are one of my preferred decorating accents, simple and beautiful. All I did was touch them up with a little blue watercolor paint.

SOAK EACH STARFISH IN A BOWL OF DYE FOR NICE, DEEP HUES.

4

SPONTANEOUS BEAUTY

ANYTIME ENTERTAINING

PREVIOUS SPREAD
I love the pale colors of this old wooden elephant. He's rare, as most similar figures tend to be painted in rather vivid colors outside my palette. I use him as a "greeter" to welcome guests to the house. I treasure him all the more because he was a gift.

OPPOSITE
My washed, creased silk tablecloth is a grounding element against formal chinaware and silvery paper doilies. Yet everything has a glittering metallic luster, from the sheen on the silk to the golden gleam of the china that radiates luxury.

Collecting is a very personal endeavor. As much as I take pleasure in beautiful objects, I really love to collect things that are useful.

That isn't to say that I don't enjoy accumulating things just because they resonate with me. I own about half a dozen things that I have acquired because they make me feel good. I have a little red leather-bound book, for instance, with beautiful paper and a lovely handwritten script in beautiful inks. There's no real use for it. It's stashed away on a bookshelf for the most part. However, from time to time, when the world's too fast, I look at it and it keeps me in the moment. Even though modern communication is faster and easier than ever before, it seems that less is being truly said. I love the thoughtfulness that these carefully handwritten words imply—that every word was meticulously chosen. I keep this book and a few other treasures because they serve a profound and soulful purpose for me, but I don't feel the need to collect little glass reindeer or other knickknacks.

I like to collect items that I can use as embellishments— simple things such as scruffy little bits of flowers, lace, or paper doilies. Not necessarily arts-and-crafts sorts of things, just small items such as napkins, brooches, and sparkling glass jewels. I find that these elements are an easy way to make something spectacular, whether they're displayed on a tray, used to decorate a card, or sprinkled on a table.

What catches my eye? Is it floral, does it have a great patina, is it in my palette? Those are the places to start. Does it have a function? I don't need a cupboard stuffed with things that I'll never use.

When you see something you like, pick it up. You never know how you might use it. I find that when I fill my life with my favorite things, there's a harmony in it. Even though I buy a lot of disparate things, because I like certain colors, shapes, and textures, they tend to work together without effort. They spontaneously form a pleasing environment. Then, when there's an occasion, you don't have to rush out or plan from scratch. You already have the advantage of a beautiful setting, because you've surrounded yourself with a lot of things you love, no matter how big or little the items might be.

Whenever you'd like to get together with a bunch of friends, you can be spontaneous because you will always have a source of decorative items. You can create a festive, playful atmosphere with very little effort. If you surround yourself with your favorite beautiful things, you don't have to decorate for a party. Don't clear the room for a gathering, use the elements in your home that are there already, whether playing cards, ribbons, or vintage chairs.

I picked up these sparkling bangle bracelets for almost nothing at a beauty supply store. Used as part of the gift wrapping, they are more than pretty enough to be appreciated on their own as a lovely gift.

Birthday Greetings

Spontaneous beauty. It's easy to give a party when you choose to live among lovely things—almost no effort is involved. Washed, unironed pieces of silk fabric cover the table, creases and all, while bright flowers are casually grouped at one end. A simple gift, wrapped in tissue with a vintage card from a thrift store, and a few cupcakes lie casually next to each other. The stark white floor contrasts with the table, the overall feel of which is pink and feminine. Yet, elements like the raw-edged fabrics, cardboard boxes, and mismatched chairs have been carefully chosen to keep the look from going too syrupy. They stop it from being too pretty, even though it's beautiful.

I think it's important to personalize things, even if just a few
guests are invited. A vintage playing card is given a hole punch
and tied to the chair with pink organza ribbon. I added the
names of my guests with a silver calligraphy pen from the crafts
store. I used aces and lower-number cards, as they tend to have
the most space to write on. This created instant nametags that
were a lot more fun than place cards.

Sweet treasures. Just dip the rim of a glass in honey and then into edible sugar sprinkles for a sparkling touch that makes any beverage festive.

I love to serve drinks and treats from overseas because I find they are often packaged in the most beautiful colors.

This table is an example of spontaneous beauty. Moreover, it's as simple as can be. All the elements—the cupcakes, the glasses, and the napkins—are things I might possibly have at my house at any time. None of them are particularly fancy, though. There are great details here, whether it's the subtle hues and patinas of the vintage paint on the chairs, antique playing cards used as name tags, or the linen and paper napkins.

I think food items are best when decorated with touches that add a very subtle texture. This can be as effortless as a generic metal plate softened with a silver doily and a silver paper cupcake holder. Edible pink crystals adorn the glassware margarita-style for another easy effect.

I enjoy serving cupcakes because they're easy to decorate in a whimsical way. They're also very practical because their beauty holds up a bit longer. Once you've taken a few slices out of a cake, it no longer looks very nice, while cupcakes continue to be attractive as long as they last.

The candles and butterflies are placed about the table to add a bit of whimsy. Similarly, the flowers are gathered together simply for a spot of color. For contrast, I put out a few pieces of ornate vintage china with gold trim. Sometimes gold can be overpowering, but used in a casual way as I did here, it merely adds a gleam.

The vintage pillows with their ruffled details are a very easy way to enhance a setting. You may not want to live with pretty little throw pillows all the time, but they're wonderful embellishments at a party. They're also a cheerful accent for a sick person if you want to prop her up in bed.

Though not planned, when placed next to each other, other details in this party decor such as the parasols, the elephant, the little Asian shoes, and the clown seemed to spontaneously convey a bit of a carnival theme. The parasols are hand painted in fabulous colors, and they're affordable—around five dollars each from a store in Chinatown. I drag them out of my garage now and again and hang them from the ceiling or make a whole pile of them like I did here.

OPPOSITE
Simple cupcakes with a few decorations couldn't be an easier treat. Yet silver baking cups, a silver doily, and a silver platter make them festive, even elegant.

ABOVE
I love the pearllike decorations on this cupcake. They make it look like a piece of jewelry.

ABOVE

Delicately ruffled baskets are topped with pale roses.
I love their sense of fragile femininity.

OPPOSITE

Paper butterflies hover above a gaily patterned glass
vase for a whimsical delight.

For me, mix-and-match seating, like this collection of vintage chairs and stools, is far preferable to a standard set of chairs. Topping them off are bright slippers and beautifully detailed throw pillows.

Vintage paper napkins, quaintly called
"paper linens" by the manufacturer, sit
next to the real thing, Irish linen napkins
in my favorite pink.

Vintage tins are both beautiful and
wonderfully functional. Flea-market
shopping has taught me that if I don't grab
them the first time around, it's unlikely I
will have the chance to do so again.

The tins are the closest things I have to a regular
collection, I suppose. I know I'm selective, so when I find one
that I really like and I know I'm really going to enjoy it, I go
ahead and buy it. I don't ponder it; I don't think, "Do I really
need it?" That's how strongly I feel about the tins. I've paid two
dollars for some of them, some have been free, and some I've
paid fifty dollars for. I always grab them if I see them in my
palette or designs. They're a particularly lovely kind of storage,
whether for jewelry or bathroom supplies. The tins also evoke a
touch of nostalgia for me, since so many of them are made in
England. They remind me of various English houses in my
childhood, where you would find cookies in one tin and tea bags
in another. The tins are also useful when it's someone's birthday
and you don't want to bother wrapping something—they make a
great gift presentation.

The little cabinet on which the tins are displayed is a piece I found recently. It's not terribly old and probably dates from between the fifties and seventies. It's a bit kitschy but I think it's so cute. The piece is definitely girly and feels like it could have come out of a roadside motel. The cabinet's the type of furniture that you do find from time to time that isn't terribly expensive. These items are not of the highest quality, but they are a fun accent.

Affordable, interesting art is another way to create spontaneous settings. If you read my first four books, you know I suggested you buy paintings only if they depict a lot of flowers. Now I've moved on to other areas. Portraits have begun to fascinate me, especially when the person is rendered in a way that gives me a sense of their history and personality. I often find that portraits tell me as much about the artist as about the model. Contemplating this subtle relationship sends me on an enjoyable reverie as I let my imagination consider all the questions that these paintings tend to evoke.

For a festive gathering, I'll go through the house and select whatever artwork seems to suit the mood of the occasion. For this pink and feminine party, I focused on the theme of unique and interesting women. I chose three paintings that I thought were particularly appropriate—a clown, a dancer, and an aristocratic lady. All the paintings were intriguing and, although clearly portraits, had a sense of mystery that made me wonder about the people depicted in them. I enjoyed the effect as I positioned them around the party room. As different as these paintings were from one another, together they created an unplanned mood of beauty and grace the way only art can.

ABOVE AND FOLLOWING PAGE
The intricate detail and subtle colors are what make vintage tins so appealing.

OPPOSITE
My pink cabinet. I discovered it on a road trip and was instantly captivated. It was perfect "as is," and I had nothing more done to it. Above hangs a fine oil painting of a clown. The original rich colors of the painting had faded into subtle soft shades that gave the work a mysterious charm. After gazing at it a while, I suddenly realized the clown was female. To this day, she inspires a contemplative mood in me as I wonder what she is thinking and where she is pointing. Her wistful appeal is unique, and I was happy to have rescued her from a New York flea market on a rainy day.

Finally, here's one last suggestion for the art of spontaneous entertaining: thorough organization. Make room for the elements you love. If you have some storage already set up, it's easy to collect inspiring items as you find them. I have boxes of flowers, a box of ribbons, and a box of papery things.

I have many drawers in my house. Yet if they're not filled with functional things I prefer they stay empty. The drawers that are stuffed are full of things that get used. I know what's in every drawer. I have a pretty good mental recollection that the little bit of shredded pink ribbon is in the top left drawer. If I need it, out it comes to decorate a package or wrap around some flowers.

I recently found a new box of tat at a flea market. *Tat* is the British word for "stuff." This is one of the most exciting finds for me. Once I've sorted through all the lovely bits of lace, vintage brooches, pastel feathers, and velvet flowers, I'll have that many more choices the next time I decide to create a spontaneous celebration.

A flock of ethereal paper-and-bamboo umbrellas light up the corner. Unique and very affordable, they have the wonderful quality of vintage pieces even though they are brand-new. The pastel colors and pretty floral designs make them perfect for my world.

5

MAGICAL
BAT MITZVAH

TWO SISTERS' SPECIAL DAY

OPPOSITE AND LEFT

I found these fab Hispanic corsages in downtown Los Angeles. Originally designed for a *quinceañera* (the coming-of-age ceremony for fifteen-year-old Latinas), the pale colors seemed perfect. Then it occurred to me to create a vintage version for the bat mitzvah bouquets. I gathered my own personal variation of the elements—small silk and velvet flowers along with velvet ribbons. Next, a hand-dyed mixture of laces and tulle was added to the mix. One bouquet was crafted in pink, one in blue. Finally, all that was needed was to transfer the plastic holder from the original *quinceañera* inspirational bouquet to my vintage versions and voilà . . . I love the result.

I've known the twins, Jennie and Sarah, for most of their lives and enjoyed watching them grow up. Therefore, I was pleased when their mother, Debra, asked me to help her plan a bat mitzvah party for the girls. Though the traditional Jewish coming-of-age ceremony has been celebrated for girls since only 1924, it's been embraced with enthusiasm as a ritual to honor a girl's entry into adulthood. Many of the festivities can be quite elaborate, and Debra was concerned because she had only a small budget to work with. She also wanted to ensure that the celebration was appropriate for the age of her girls. Debra thought an informal event for family and friends would be best. I assured Debra that we could come up with something that was every bit as fun and beautiful as a more lavish party by focusing on personal touches that would be meaningful to the girls.

A few days later, Jennie and Sarah came to my house, and we sat together and talked. I asked about their favorite colors and interests. I wanted the girls to be involved and help me incorporate things that really reflected their interests and meant something to them.

They told me about the basic elements of the religious ceremony and the party afterward. We would need prayer shawls, invitations, place settings, and tables with lavish centerpieces. I considered these traditional elements and began to think of ways to translate them into my world. This was great fun for the girls. Jennie and Sarah love Shabby Chic, have watched me do little arts-and-crafts projects over the years, and have always seemed to enjoy them and connect with them.

After talking with the girls, I knew that the themes for the bat mitzvah would be art and ballet and that Jennie's favorite color was blue and Sarah's was green. However, I really didn't have any specific ideas yet, so I decided to go downtown for inspiration. With shops featuring goods from all over the world, including China, India, and Mexico, it's hard not to get motivated. Looking at unusual items from other countries and cultures, with their exotic colors, shapes, and patterns, is always a delight for me. I knew that something would catch my eye and suggest a creative way to approach the bat mitzvah party.

To my delight, I found several stores that specialized in accessories and decorations for the *quinceañera*. A Hispanic tradition, the *quinceañera* is a commemoration of a girl's fifteenth birthday—the coming-of-age ceremony for that culture. The celebration traditionally begins with a religious ceremony and is followed by a reception in the home or a banquet hall. I was struck by the similarity of the Hispanic and Jewish rituals in combining religious and family celebrations for a rite of passage. Jennie and Sarah had studied very hard for the bat mitzvah ceremony at the synagogue. The party following later that evening would be a reward for their efforts and an opportunity to relax and have fun.

The *quinceañera* stores inspired me. They were filled with glass goblets engraved with ribbons and flowers, ornate corsages, and colorful printed napkins. I realized that by creating a vintage version of these customary Hispanic elements, I would have some great ideas for Jennie and Sarah's bat mitzvah. It was fun to mix and match these different cultural symbols and customs. It made me realize how universal the celebration of a girl's transition to womanhood truly is.

OPPOSITE

Sparkling details like the jeweled hatpin make the bat mitzvah bouquet truly special. There is something irresistible about such a pretty, gleaming trinket tucked among fresh, radiant blooms.

ABOVE

Sarah and Jennie . . . holding their vintage bat mitzvah bouquet. A bat mitzvah is the Jewish coming-of-age ceremony for thirteen-year-old girls.

There are many components for a bat mitzvah invitation: the invitation for the ceremony itself, one for the party afterward, directions to the synagogue and to the festivities, and so forth. Consequently, several different sheets had to be designed. For Jennie and Sarah, I gathered together small patches of Shabby Chic fabric, ribbons, and flowers in the girls' favorite colors of green and blue. They were assembled into a collage on a piece of card stock. The result was lovely but not slick, with a homemade, arts-and-crafts feel to the invitations.

I made these photo collage boards and set them up on rented easels at the entrance to the party so that the guests could learn all about Jennie and Sarah. One board focused on Jennie, one on Sarah, while a third and fourth board focused on friends and family. Their mother contributed a wonderful collection of pictures, but rather than cut them up and stick pins through them, I photocopied them all. Some pictures were blown up; others were colorized or converted to black-and-white. To give the feeling of a scrapbook, I also added vintage flowers, personal letters, and collected programs and memorabilia.

INVITATIONS

It's important that invitations convey a sense of anticipation and excitement the moment they arrive. They should give some hint of the tone or theme of the upcoming festivities, as well as the facts of when and where. I like them to be as personal as possible. When the guest list is small enough, I make each invitation myself and address it by hand. However, for larger occasions when that's simply not practical, I still try to make the invitations look as homemade as possible. Little additions like a ribbon, flowers, rhinestones, and feathers make an enormous difference. When invitations are sent with care, guests happily suspect that the party will be special as well.

Our family joyfully invites you
to join us when

Jennie and Sarah

are called to the Torah as
B'not Mitzvah
_y, the second of November
_ thousand and two
_ in the morning
Kehillat Israel
16019 Sunset Boulevard
Pacific Palisades, California

Kiddush following the service

Deborah, Sarah and Jennie

TENT
DECORATIONS

When it came time to assemble all my elements and decorate for the party, I was fortunate to have the help of my friend Theresa. Even though I had certain visions for the party and had collected certain items, I needed Theresa to help pull it all together because I simply didn't have enough time to do it all myself. Theresa was able to fill in the blanks both practically and creatively, and I couldn't have done it without her.

I rented a basic party tent and put it up in the backyard, because the event was held in November and the weather can be

One of the lovely paintings Jennie has created over the years.

The moments before a party always seem a little bit magical, but it's especially true here. The delicate pastel colors and twinkling fairy lights give an ethereal quality to the tented setting. Tulle wrapped around the table and tied in bows on the chairs gives a whimsical, almost theatrical, touch as it evokes the idea of ballerinas gliding across a stage. Though a bit different from a conventional bat mitzvah party, all the decorative details from fans to flowers are sweetly feminine as is appropriate for two young girls celebrating their transition to womanhood.

a bit dodgy at that time of year. I didn't mind, though, because tents are also a wonderful way to create a separate, more intimate world for a party. However, because of their size, tents can be tricky to decorate on a budget. I gathered some fabric into swags using a slightly more intense version of our blue-and-green palette, with violet as an accent, so that the draped fabric would show up against the white tent. More fabric and strands of fairy lights disguised the tent's metal support frame, and ribbon was wound around many of the tent poles. The result was that the practical metal poles were now multicolored, resembling those on a merry-go-round. The sturdy tent now seemed light and delicate, shimmering with touches of color.

TABLES
AND CHAIRS

I rented tables and chairs for the party. I deliberately chose simple chairs that would easily lend themselves to decoration. The tables were placed end-to-end in two long rows. Instead of conventional tablecloths, I wanted something more whimsical and frivolous. For a few dollars, I found some long rolls of plastic sheeting in blue and cream. It actually felt more youthful to me to cover the rented tables that way, so I was pleased with my discovery.

Because part of the theme was ballet, I had skirts made for the tables out of tulle and attached them to the plastic tablecloths in a way that suggested a ballerina's tutu. I stayed within my palette and used pale greens, blues, and lilacs.

Tulle is a fantastic fabric. Easily found in great colors, affordable and whimsical, it was my choice for the party. Tulle can make anything lovely and festive, so I bought yards and yards of it, using it at every opportunity.

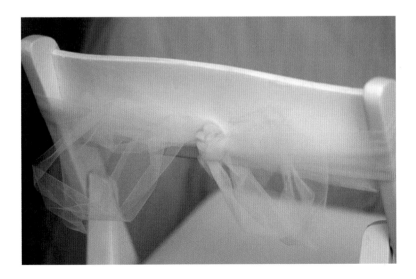

OPPOSITE AND LEFT
Tying simple tulle bows around the standard rented chairs made them instantly festive.

TOP

Enhancing a plastic tablecloth with tulle is the perfect combination of beauty, budget, and function.

CENTER

Plastic tablecloths provided the base. Tulle was then gathered together with a needle and thread.

BOTTOM

The gathered tulle skirt was attached to the plastic with a glue gun.

OPPOSITE

I used some lovely vintage trim to hide the joins and any unsightly staples or glue, and also for extra decoration.

CENTERPIECES

The centerpieces continued the themes of ballet and art. The ballet has always been very dear to my heart. I love the details of tulle on the tutus and the ribbons on the satin ballet shoes—and they're often my favorite color, pink, as well.

Theresa and I began designing three ballet centerpieces by first laying out all the different elements. We looked at everything from classic toe shoes to cheap little plastic ballerina dolls. We brainstormed how to use the different pieces, including vintage flowers, bits of cloth, lace, beads, and so on. It was necessary to look at these elements in a new and original way, because the ballet theme can easily become a cliché. I wanted the centerpieces to look charming and unique rather than predictable. For example, I'd found a beautiful turquoise rhinestone tiara, and Theresa had the wonderful idea to use the tiara as part of the bodice and center of a miniature tutu in a centerpiece.

One of the most imaginative centerpieces involved a pair of pale pink satin ballet shoes strapped to a Styrofoam cone wrapped in turquoise velvet ribbon in a braided pattern. The whole thing rests on a cloud of tulle gathered into a sparkling bejeweled tiara in a way that suggests the delicate skirt of a tutu.

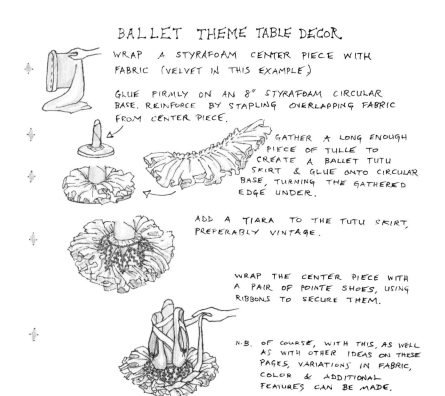

BALLET THEME TABLE DECOR

WRAP A STYRAFOAM CENTER PIECE WITH FABRIC (VELVET IN THIS EXAMPLE.)

GLUE FIRMLY ON AN 8" STYRAFOAM CIRCULAR BASE. REINFORCE BY STAPLING OVERLAPPING FABRIC FROM CENTER PIECE.

GATHER A LONG ENOUGH PIECE OF TULLE TO CREATE A BALLET TUTU SKIRT & GLUE ONTO CIRCULAR BASE, TURNING THE GATHERED EDGE UNDER.

ADD A TIARA TO THE TUTU SKIRT, PREFERABLY VINTAGE.

WRAP THE CENTER PIECE WITH A PAIR OF POINTE SHOES, USING RIBBONS TO SECURE THEM.

N.B. OF COURSE, WITH THIS, AS WELL AS WITH OTHER IDEAS ON THESE PAGES, VARIATIONS IN FABRIC, COLOR & ADDITIONAL FEATURES CAN BE MADE.

ABOVE

I can easily find a multitude of uses for my beloved flower kebabs. Moreover, they're easy—just a length of wire strung with bits and bobs, including mercury beads, plastic beads, and vintage flowers that I found at the flea market. The key is to use the most beautiful elements you can find.

LEFT

Inexpensive plastic dolls were transformed into prima ballerinas with a little gold paint.

OPPOSITE

The "prima ballerina" centerpiece . . . another toy ballerina in the most eye-catching presentation of all—standing atop a platform constructed from a Styrofoam circle and half a Styrofoam ball covered with pink cotton and lace, beautifully trimmed with delicious vintage flowers and leaves. I inserted a couple of the flower kebabs for added height and drama.

Nearly every little girl has been entranced by a dancing ballerina jewelry box at some point in her childhood. Though they're slightly kitschy, I found this one irresistible and was inspired to use the little jewelry case as a creative starting point to develop the theme of several centerpieces for the party.

BELOW

All this centerpiece required was placing a ballerina on a little ruffled box. The pink crepe confection came from my "one day I will use . . ." cupboard.

OPPOSITE

This centerpiece was put together using a velvet-and-pearl pincushion, a small bunch of forget-me-nots, and one of the toy ballerinas, complete with tutu.

142

ART THEME TABLE DECOR

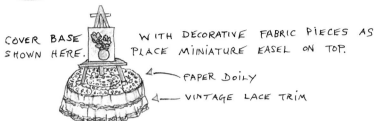

- GLUE TOGETHER THREE 8" STYRAFOAM DISCS

- COVER BASE SHOWN HERE. WITH DECORATIVE FABRIC PIECES AS PLACE MINIATURE EASEL ON TOP.
  - ◁—— PAPER DOILY
  - ◁—— VINTAGE LACE TRIM

- COLLECT OBJECTS THAT RELATE TO THE ACTIVITY OF PAINTING :—

- ASSEMBLE THEM ON & AROUND EASEL AS DEMONSTRATED IN PHOTO OF FINISHED PIECE.

A masterpiece for the table, this centerpiece consists of an easel with a little oil painting of flowers, a used palette colored with dabs of paint, a bottle of ink, tubes of paint, and brushes—all hand painted and coordinated to match the color scheme. Everything is then secured on a platform of painted Styrofoam and lace. It's the perfect representation of Jennie's love of art.

The art-themed centerpieces were handled a little differently. The idea was to create three-dimensional paintings for the table—compositions that clearly looked like still lifes, with vases and some flowers in actual picture frames. Working within my color scheme, I chose suitable colors for the paints and the chalks that were added as part of the centerpieces—a joy when you have all the tones of an artist's palette to work from.

Of course, as with most table displays, I did have some floral arrangements. I used simple glass vases, and I made sure they were short because I wanted the kids to be able to talk to each other over them. I put one hydrangea bloom in each vase.

Classic still life collection: a variety of petite vintage vases filled with fresh flowers, framed and set on painted Styrofoam circles covered in silver doilies.

PLACE SETTINGS

Place settings for children and young teens need to be both pretty and practical. However, that's no reason to compromise. I'm a firm believer in the charm of everyday elements. Paper, plastic, cardboard, aluminum foil, and drinking straws all have wonderful potential. Kitschy, exuberant colors and materials that might be out of place at an adult function can be given free rein here. Used with imagination, they can be transformed into magical place settings at a table set in the fantasy-rich world of the young.

OPPOSITE

A feather and ribbon gave the same jazzy touch to the plastic cutlery. I love this look.

LEFT

Paper napkins, personalized with the girls' names and the date of the bat mitzvah, were highly coveted. Many party supply stores offer personalized napkins, and they can be quite affordable. Simple things like this are often kept forever as treasured mementos.

The party was a great success. Jennie and Sarah really loved the fact that it was done by me in a very personal way, rather than by a professional party planner. I really liked the fact that although it was simply done, the final result was ethereal. The setting took on a life of its own with the delicate ribbons, the clear plastic tableware decorated with feathers, and the tulle bows on the chairs. Everything seemed slightly magical. It never would have happened with real china and crystal, and it wasn't just "making do." Jennie and Sarah's bat mitzvah party ended up having a special quality that even a very expensive catered affair couldn't duplicate.

Paper plates and bowls are all that's needed for an informal kid's party, but silver crowns stamped on each dish made it look fresh and personal. This ended up being one of my very favorite touches.

Using regular glassware at a party for young teens seemed neither safe nor practical. To keep it fun, however, I purchased a pack of fifty plastic champagne glasses and added a ribbon on each stem.

BOTTOM RIGHT

Another Hispanic inspiration was the *quinceañera copa,* traditionally used to toast the occasion. The etched calligraphy and pretty ribbon trim encouraged me to try my own version.

OPPOSITE

A simple etching kit from an arts-and-crafts store was used to trace Jennie and Sarah's initials onto plain wineglasses, transforming them into keepsake goblets. A final addition of turquoise feathers, also from the arts-and-crafts store, along with lavender ribbons, and I was done.

6

IT'S ALL IN
THE DETAILS

FINAL
THOUGHTS

My crème de la crème table. Though suitable for a gala event and the most sumptuous venue, I placed the elaborate table in a simple room with pure white walls. A sense of intimacy is achieved with rented stanchions that define the space. I made them my own by covering the usual red ropes with slips in pink crushed velvet. A stunning ruffled tablecloth of slightly creased muslin and lace is the first of many details that give the rented round table an air of royal extravagance. Majestic silver crowns are found upon the table along with whimsical pink-feathered halos. Both were inexpensive finds at a party-supply store. Gleaming gold chargers from a home store are the platform for the china, which is a mix of the regal and the commonplace—vintage china and plain white restaurant ware. Vintage cranberry glassware completes the place settings. A cement urn is a pleasingly solid contrast to an ornate centerpiece of delicate ostrich feathers and lush violet roses. Finally, antique French chairs from a treasured set I bought years ago are the last touch, topped with white linen slipcovers whose ruffles echo the look of the tablecloth.

A silver crown provides a regal accent against ivory lace, while a golden coronet is the luminous highlight of the exquisite china pattern found on a vintage plate in this majestic place setting. A gleaming gold charger ties the elements together. As opulent as this gilded finery looks, the crown and charger were inexpensive finds that nevertheless add a great deal of beauty, not to mention fun, to the occasion.

There is one common thread in all the parties, settings, and celebrations in this book, and that is a meticulous attention to detail. Each element is as beautiful as it can be. Even though I may start with basics like tables, chairs, and china, I always find it pays to reinvent these essentials by using a unique table treatment, mixing and matching the china, or decorating the chairs. These touches make all the difference. Sometimes it's about things that you don't even see, the little hidden details that aren't obvious but make something feel so complete, high quality, and cared for . . . the ribbon on a name tag or a bit of sparkling vintage trim that hides a staple. Quality is not necessarily about dollar value. It is being confident that, no matter from which angle you view your creation, it looks good. Quality is about pride and knowing you've done something properly. If you're going to bother doing something, do it well from beginning to end.

A noble-looking cement urn in a classical style lends an air of stately dignity to a rather playful arrangement of turquoise feathers and pink roses. The juxtaposition of the substantial urn and the delicate feathers and flowers makes for an unexpectedly graceful centerpiece. The deep cranberry color of the vintage glasses sets off all the lovely muted colors of the table.

OPPOSITE

Whimsical luxury is the theme of this place setting with a pink feathered halo, a lace napkin in luscious crème de la crème pink, topped off by a velvety vintage flower and a glittering brooch. Pink jewels set against the creamy metal setting of the brooch are a gorgeous combination.

Nowhere is this more apparent than in my most elegant and luxurious table of all. This is the crème de la crème of tables for me. Beautifully set, carefully arranged, and skillfully lit, this regal table is really no more—or less—than a painstaking assemblage of detail after detail. Moreover, it is surprisingly affordable, a lavish champagne treat on a beer budget.

One simple way to achieve elegance, no matter what the budget, is through the use of color. I use my classic palette but choose those hues at the subtle end of its spectrum. The muted values of my palette determine the mood. Pink and blue can be bright and youthful, but when the same colors are toned down, they take on a more elegant and demure aura. They are beautiful in a subdued way. I kept this in mind when selecting all the pieces to display on the table, from rhinestone brooches to roses.

Everyone loves a taste of luxury now and then, the chance to play at being a bit grand. However, few really enjoy an unrelentingly formal affair. Whimsical touches like feather halos and silver crowns brighten up a refined occasion. They spark entertaining conversations at the table, helping people feel less self-conscious. It makes a traditional event less predictable. Nevertheless, there is still a sense of the occasion with beautiful elements such as the luminous clear-glass reproduction chandelier. As loyal as I am to vintage pieces, there are such good affordable reproductions available that I can't resist using them. Other luxurious accents include a generously ruffled, albeit wrinkled, tablecloth and sumptuous place settings. Together with such innovative touches as pastel feathers and jeweled napkin rings, all this attention to detail upon detail culminates in a table that, for me, is absolutely glorious, a virtual symphony of celebration.

No detail is too small to be worthy of your best efforts. An ongoing effort to surround yourself with beauty enhances your life. Buy the prettiest grocery store items you can find. A colorful water bottle or lemonade drink brightens the day. Invest in the lovely little accessories of life.

ABOVE AND OPPOSITE

It's so important to think creatively and not to overlook any possibility. I was in the Covent Garden Hotel in London when I fell in love with this particular bottle because of its turquoise color. I decided that I had to bring some home and use them for a party. I wanted to personalize the bottle somehow and decided to get out my rubber stamps and some silver inkpads and spell out H_2O on a small tag. I really enjoyed the project even though there were thirty bottles that had to have the label steamed off, thirty little H_2O stamps to make, and thirty ribbons to tie on. When doing repetitive crafts, I do find that the first few are kind of my learning curve. On the first few H_2O tags I did, the $_2$ was a little wonky and the O was too big, but by the last ten tags, I had it down. I actually find the whole process therapeutic and a way to really master something. So now I'm the perfect H_2O tag person.

LEFT

Develop an eye for detail and be on the lookout for the perfect found object. These pink lemonade bottles are exactly as I bought them at the grocery store. The shape, colors, and design couldn't work better for my world.

Flowers are perhaps the most exquisite detail of all. Endlessly versatile, they enrich my soul and inspire my sense of beauty. I love flowers that look as though they just came from the garden, casual yet perfect. The contrived perfection of hothouse flowers is not for me. I prefer arrangements that are not too precious, arrangements that look as if I've just gone outside and gathered my favorites. Options for flower containers are practically limitless, as long as they hold water. I like to assemble glass jars, cement urns, watering cans, and vintage pitchers, just for a start. I often arrange vases or bowls into interesting collections and group them by color, shape, or materials. Usually, the more stunning the container, the fewer flowers that are needed, which is especially helpful when working on a budget.

Simple bouquets can be tied together
with ribbon and attached to the backs of
chairs for a wedding dinner or any special
occasion. It's a lovely detail.

Amy Neunsinger, a close friend and talented photographer, has worked with me on several books. We share an appreciation for form, light, and color and a fondness for lovely things, especially flowers. Amy got married on a farm outside Savannah, Georgia, in a simple barefoot wedding that was nevertheless extremely beautiful, and united family and friends in a heartfelt celebration. The flowers were central to the spirit of the occasion, and I couldn't resist the opportunity to share several lovely examples in this book.

OPPOSITE AND LEFT
All the wedding arrangements were simple, homemade, and completely charming. This kept the focus of the day where it should be—on the bride and groom and their brand new marraige.

A large magnolia bloom lies resplendent in a shallow cream bowl. It radiates the dignity of a beautiful piece of sculpture.

Since guests were encouraged to go barefoot at the wedding, aluminum washtubs were filled with warm water and an armful of peonies and roses. It looked absolutely wonderful. Guests who dipped their toes in the water felt completely pampered.

The wedding lasted the whole weekend. This meant that there were different functions—the rehearsal dinner, morning breakfast, and wedding dinner—that all needed different flowers. Wildflowers were collected along with roses, lilies, magnolias, and dahlias. Miniature bowls and numerous other containers were called into service. Volunteers under the supervision of Amy's mother, Carol, lovingly put everything from little corsages to a rose wreath together. The result was a simple country wedding with a subtle sophistication rivaling the most elaborate ceremony. I've often drawn upon the floral arrangements of this beautiful celebration as an inspiration for other occasions.

My favorite flowers are uncomplicated and natural, with a sense of innocence and fresh beginnings. There are so many flowers with beautiful lacy ruffled shapes, such as garden roses, lisianthus, and peonies, that are perfect for a wedding or other celebration without unnecessary embellishment. Of course, my usual color palette of pale pastels and creams fits in especially well with a wedding theme. However, while the arrangements might be simple, be as lavish as you like with the amount of flowers you use. If you love them as I do, enjoy any chance to indulge your passion with an abundance of flowers.

A monochromatic arrangement of different flowers in the same lilac hue is stunning in a simple glass vase.

For a unique floral treatment, scatter a variety of miniature bowls all over the table. Some of these are made of marble or porcelain, while others are fashioned out of seashells. Then just put a single bud in every one. It's all that's needed.

Frilly peonies, lacy lisianthus,
and delicate sweet peas
provide a feast for the eye.

While spending some time at the hospital, I ran across standard institutional trays. To bring them into my world, I began with a paper doily and then added a beautifully embroidered white hanky with a little pink ribbon around it. I added a lovely white eggcup in gold paisley print that I found at the flea market and a Moroccan glass with a white design. This breakfast tray would be a wonderful way to begin anyone's day. The tray is really beautiful, and there's nothing there that's less than dazzling. In its own way, it's perfect.

Plain dinner trays are set in a row for
a wedding rehearsal dinner. Easy and
practical for an informal family gathering,
they are nevertheless surprisingly elegant
when lined up on a long row of tables
covered with white paper. Crayons are
available in clear plastic cups for anyone
who feels the setting needs further
decoration. Small wildflowers are stuffed
into jam jars. The arrangement is
unpretentious and very pretty.

I was impressed not only by the flowers at Amy's wedding
but also by her use of plastic trays during the rehearsal dinner.
In keeping with Amy's plan for a family-style affair, she offered
a casual evening event with an affordable, fun dinner. Plain
dinner trays like those you'd find in a church or school were
used. However, with embellishments such as cutlery tied
together with string and lovely wildflowers in jam jars, they
became something special.

The uncomplicated charm of Amy's dinner trays inspired
me. It made me aware of the possibilities of using such
utilitarian and rather pedestrian items as a tableau on which to
create a small still life of beautiful objects, and I keep my eyes
open for the sweet accessories and fancy touches that will
complement such a setting. This is part of a larger ongoing

Have a sweet night

OPPOSITE
Surprise houseguests with a special treat before they turn in. Scatter flower petals on the bed and top it with a plate that holds Oreo cookies and a little metal bucket with ice and a glass of milk. An attached note wishes everyone a nice night.

LEFT
There is something particularly charming when every detail is perfect on an especially diminutive accessory. This candle is just over two inches high and nestled in a petite candy foil among tiny colorful beads. There is no better way to show your commitment to quality.

search of mine: I am always in pursuit of the ideal detail. These items will make or break my efforts, so everything I use is subject to intense scrutiny. Since less is more, less has to be perfect. Every detail carries a message, and it has to do so with clarity and purpose. Is an object pretty, regal, whimsical, or sentimental? Does it exist just as a symbol of pure beauty? I'm selective. These objects carry the weight of my intent. The success of any party or celebration is dependent on these carefully chosen items, along with how and where they are displayed. A delicate flower may need the support of a heavy stone urn in order to find its voice, while a large, beautiful bud deserves to shine on its own in a small unassuming vase. Though your setting may be a quiet corner or a spectacular venue at the center of everything, it is the details that will make it perfect, unique, and beautiful.

Handmade signs that spell out EAT ME and DRINK ME are a whimsical touch at a tea party for grown-up Alices.

This table is set buffet-style with assorted pretty blue glasses from a selection in my store, some vintage, some new. The combination of new glasses with vintage makes for a more interesting presentation—as does mixing vintage china with some plastic plates. The whole idea of mixing vintage pieces with ordinary materials like plastic, paper, or cardboard is very appealing to me. The everyday items bring vintage's formal, elaborate look down to earth, while the vintage elements dress up the basics.

A frilly feminine cake . . . it only takes minutes to put together with layers of icing, meringue cookies, and flowers.

The whole idea of mixing vintage pieces with ordinary materials like plastic, paper, or cardboard is very appealing to me. The everyday items bring vintage's formal, elaborate look down to earth, while the vintage elements dress up the basics.

This place setting is quintessentially me in design. All my essential details are there, including mismatched china in graceful floral patterns, a puckered muslin tablecloth, vintage glasses with delicate gold trim, and ornate silverware. Single flower buds are slipped into small bowls and lace-trimmed napkins. And of course, there are sweetly scented candles.

I've carried this birdbath from home to home in my many moves. Sometimes
I let it just sit there filled with water for the birds, but other times, especially
when I have company, I like to fling in a few roses. The turquoise patina at
the bottom of the basin is an added incentive to toss flowers into it, as the
color sets them off so beautifully.

RESOURCE GUIDE

SHABBY CHIC CORPORATE OFFICES
shabbychic.com
6330 Arizona Circle
Los Angeles, CA 90045
Phone: (310) 670-9083

RACHEL ASHWELL SHABBY CHIC
shabbychic.com
Locations:

> 1013 Montana Avenue
> Santa Monica, CA 90403
> Phone: (310) 394-1975

> 3095 Sacramento Street
> San Francisco, CA 94115
> Phone: (415) 929-2990

> 5808 Wagner Road
> Round Top, TX 78954
> Phone: (979) 836-4975

> 83 Wooster Street
> New York, NY 10012
> Phone: (212) 334-3500

> 202 Kensington Park Road
> London, England W11 1NR
> Phone: (+44) 20 77929022

For bedding, furniture, décor, accessories,
and gifts as seen in this book.

TARGET
target.com
Visit website for locations.
"Simply Shabby Chic" line of bedding, curtains,
and furniture slipcovers from Rachel Ashwell sold
exclusively through Target, in store and online.

ROSE LANE FARMS
11740 Sherman Way
North Hollywood, CA 91605
Phone: (323) 791-1367
E-mail: roselanefarms@fbcglobal.net
Flowers for baby shower

MICHAELS
michaels.com
Visit website for locations.

MAPLE CRAFT
925 South Maple Avenue
Los Angeles, CA 90015
Phone: 1-800-842-0633
Arts-and-crafts supplies, quinceanera bouquets and glasses,
fans, plastic tablecloths, miniature booties, ballerina dolls,
custom-printed ribbons, baby shower signs.

MICHAEL LEVINE
lowpricefabric.com
920 Maple Avenue
Los Angeles, CA 90015
Phone: (213) 622-6259
Fabrics, trim

ROSE BOWL FLEA MARKET
rosebowlstadium.com/events/flea-market
1001 Rose Bowl Drive
Pasadena, CA 91103
Phone: (323) 560-7469
Second Sunday of every month: vintage clothes, accessories,
used furniture, and crafts.

SMART & FINAL
smartandfinal.com
To locate nearest California store please
call toll-free 1-800-894-0511
Aluminum take-out containers

CHROME HEARTS
chromehearts.com
870 Madison Avenue
New York, NY 10021
Phone: (212) 794-3100
Leather bags

600 North Robertson Boulevard
Los Angeles, CA 90069
Phone: (310) 854-9800
Also locations in Las Vegas, Honolulu, Malibu, Europe, and Asia.

. . . one stitch at a time.